Everything I say is true, true and again true

FOR MY HUSBAND

AUTHOR / COVER / IMAGES

TANJA M. FEILER

PART I

13 YEARS OF MARRIAGE

PART 1: REPORT / COLLECTION

2002 - 2006

▯ PROFESSIONAL LIFE
▯ SOCIAL INVOLVEMENT IN THE PRIVATE SECTOR
▯ "WE CHILDREN OF THE WORLD" THE INTERN. BUCHMARKT
▯ 2003 BEGINS THE ERA OF AMOROUS WOMEN

2006 - 2011

LOST ▯ PROFESSIONAL
▯ DISEASE
▯ THE SYSTEM OF HARTZ 4
▯ PENSION APPLICATIONS, REFUSALS
▯ FRIENDS - NIGHTMARE
▯ BUILD INDEPENDENCE

▯ DOCUMENTED: EXPERIENCES

4

TO UNDERSTAND
☐ NIGHTMARE WOMEN
☐ NEW DRUG ELONTRIL,
ANTIDEPRESSANT - THE
PRESSED EVERYTHING OUT OF
THE PERSONALITY

2011 - CAUSALITY - I'M TALKING
ABOUT ME:

- THE PRIMARY PERSONALITY
REMAINS INTACT, BUT NOT AN
ESCAPE FROM YOURSELF
POSSIBLE. FREEDOM LEADS TO

5

EGOISM, FLAME BODY IMAGE MEANS THAT I BECOME PROSTITUTES "WANTED". EIGHT YEARS BETWEEN TOTAL FIXATION ON MY HUSBAND, AND IDOLATRY SIMPLY DESPITE VOWS TO BREAK IT. HAVING SPENT FOUR DAYS WITH ANOTHER PERSON, MY HUSBAND HAS PHOTOGRAPHED ME. I WAS APPALLED. JUST LIKE THIS MAN WAS MY VIEW, DISGUSTING. MY HUSBAND SAVED ME FROM CERTAIN DOOM TO AS A HOOKER. TWO MONTHS LATER, I HAD SEX WITH TWO MEN - I DID NOT PREVIOUSLY, I JUST WENT TO A "DEVOTEE" OF THE INTERNET, HAD A VISIT FROM HIS BROTHER. THIS EXPERIENCE I HAVE DESCRIBED IN "THE FOG OF NOWHERE", AND IN THE POETRY BOOK STANTE PEDE DETAIL. COLD - I GOT THE ROLE OF A PORN ACTRESS PLAYED- THE NEXT DAY REPORTED MY SOUL, PAIN, I RETURNED HOME

WITHOUT ASKING ME THE PAIN - BUT MADE TO COOL. MONTHS WENT BY, IT WAS THE SAME AS BEFORE 2011: NO THOUGHTS OF OTHER MEN. THROUGH THE EXPERIENCE OF COLD - NO PORN. MOVIES I LOOK AT MORE, DOING MY SOUL HURT - YES GIRL. AS A CHILD I ALSO EXPERIENCED SOMETHING "PARANORMAL" - BELIEVING TO GOD -

IN SEPTEMBER 2011, MY HUSBAND AND I RENEWED OUR VOWS. FOR ETERNITY. BUT HOW TO LIVE WITH THE GUILT? MY HUSBAND HAS NEVER BROKEN HIS PROMISE.

THE HONESTY, TRUST, KNOWLEDGE OF THE TRUTH ARE THE BASIC REQUIREMENTS. IN JULY 2012, MY HUSBAND TOLD ME OF A CONVERSATION

THAT I HAD DONE WITH THE PEOPLE, WITH WHOM I LIVED IN 2011 A FEW DAYS. FOUR DAYS OF MISTRUST - THEN I WENT TO THE TABLE TO GET FOOD AND SUDDENLY I SEE SAID PEOPLE ARE MIDDLE OF THE ROOM - SHOCK - WHEN I GO HOME, AND DIRK REPORTS, WHO I MET AT THE TABLE, THEN MY HUSBAND ASK ME WHAT WE TALKED ABOUT - WHAT I'VE BEEN TOLD FOUR DAYS TO MEET WITH THE SAID PERSON HAD THUS COME TRUE. IF I MAKE THE DECISION TO IGNORE THESE PEOPLE, THEN MY HUSBAND WILL SAY THAT I'M A COWARD AND NOT STAND BY WHAT MY HUSBAND THINKS YES TO KNOW EH. IT SEEMED LIKE HOURS BEFORE, WHERE I WAITED FOR THE BOARD - WHAT SHOULD I DO? ACTION. I LET OUT A SMALL KNIFE IN HIS SHOULDER AND RAN HOME. TOLD ALL FEAR, DISBELIEF ... AND TODAY THERE IS A

PRESENTATION OF THE TRUTH: I HAVE THEREFORE COME TO THE MAN THE KNIFE INTO THE SHOULDER, BECAUSE I DO NOT WANT TO BE LIKE MY FATHER AND ME NOT GUILTY DO WITH THE MAN - TO HAVE GUILTY AS, AGREED, MY KILLING MAN.
THAT IS NOT TRUE!

TODAY EASTER IS AROUND THE CORNER - SINCE 2013 I WRITE - I USE MY PRIMARY PERSONALITY, MY HUMANITY + EXPERIENCES CAUSALITY THINK PROFESSIONAL EXPERIENCE, BOTH AS A THERAPIST, AS WELL AS THROUGH THE SCIENTIFIC WORK AT THE NEWSPAPER TO CAN EXPLAIN ON AN OBJECTIVE LEVEL THROUGH COLLECTION OF

FACTS. I AM 13 YEARS, THE
PERSON WHO KNOWS
EVERYTHING, LISTEN TO,
ANALYZE -
THE POISON IS OFTEN DISTRUST
PREVENTS CLARIFICATION, BUT IT
IS SO, THE MORE I TALK, THE
WORSE IT IS.

I HAVE BEFORE I MET MY
HUSBAND, PAST IMMEDIATELY
PACKED INTO A RARORDNER -
DETERMINES A FORM OF
REPRESSION, CAUSALITIES -
UNDERSTAND THE BASICS AND
THEN NO LONGER BOTHERED
ME. MY HUSBAND, 28 YEARS
OF TORTURE BEHIND - BY
PEOPLE AND NATURE - USED TO
GET LITTLE EXPLANATION, BUT
NOTES BE SEEN TO AGREE TO
STATEMENTS OF OTHER PEOPLE
THEMSELVES.
THAT IS HUMAN, BUT HE IS
AWARE OF THE PLANET, IS
ANTHROPOLOGIST, CREATOR -

EVERYTHING CAN BE USED FOR
AND AGAINST YOU ...

PRAYER - ADDRESSED TO GOD
AND MY HUSBAND -

GOD I BEG YOU, PLEASE HELF
US THAT WE HAVE FOUR DAYS
OF VACATION.

AMEN

PART 2: WHAT DO I KNOW, WANT AND THINK - WITH EXPLANATION AND FACTS OCCUPANCY

YESTERDAY I GAVE A WOMAN MONEY BECAUSE THEY DID NOT HAVE ONE. HOW IS MY HUSBAND REACT? HE WAS ANGRY, HE SAID: IF ANYONE OUT THERE WANTS 200 EUROS, YOU CAN GIVE IT TO HIM, YES. WE HAVE EVEN LESS MONEY, BUT HE HAS ALSO GIVEN PEOPLE MONEY BECAUSE THEY HAVE ASKED HIM. HELP EACH OTHER - THAT'S NORMAL. BEFORE I WENT TO DINNER, WE TALKED ABOUT CHARITY EVENTS IN HOLLYWOOD THAT AN IMPORTANT PSYCHL. PURPOSE OF THE STARS ARE: TOGETHER, BE COMMITTED TO SOZ THING SO AS NOT TO FEEL GUILTY.. OTHERWISE WOULD MR. GATES DONATE GO EVERY DAY ... THERE ARE AVRIL - IT BELONGS

TO THE FAMILY - SHE HAS HER OWN FOUNDATION, BUT FIRST SHE HAS ALSO EG FOR AMNESTY INTERNATIONAL. WORKED. IF THE STING OF SUSPICION NOT BE POISON SPRAY, HE WOULD HAVE TAKEN ME IN HIS ARMS AND SAID VERY LOOSE: LOOK TANYA, WHAT YOU'VE GOT EVERYTHING FROM THE BOARD TODAY THAT IS WORTH THE MONEY. REPENT, VERONIKA S. BECAUSE I HAVE SINNED FOR THE FIRST TIME. BACK WHEN WE WERE STUDYING WITH THE MORMONS, I HAD TO CRY BECAUSE DIRK WANTED TO GO AWAY WITH ANOTHER. BUT I WENT WITH. WE DO NOT NEED CHURCH CONNECTION. THE WHITE DIRK FIRSTHAND, AT LEAST NOT TO JOIN ANY. I KNOW WHY HE CONFRONTED ME WITH MY TRANSGRESSIONS, ALL STILL SO DISGUSTING HUMAN WEAKNESSES CONSIDERING AND

13

SAYS: MAYBE YOU THINK, TOO, THAT .... OF COURSE, I REALIZE THAT I BRUSH MISTAKES OVER AND OVER AGAIN HOW BAD DO OR EVERYTHING WILL FIX AND DO NOT DO IT. DUE TO THE COOLNESS, JUST TIME TO GO TO A STRANGER 2011 WILL EVEN SUPPORT FROM THE HUSBAND - WHERE'S MY PRIMARY PERSONALITY? IT'S THERE. HELP IS SINCE CHILDHOOD NORMAL FOR ME, BUT I HAVE, UNLIKE DIRK, HUMAN DISAPPOINTMENTS ONLY NOW FOUND SUCH AS WHEN I WAS 16 YEARS OLD AND WAS SUBORDINATED TO ME, I HAVE A NECKLACE STOLEN, ELIZABETH AND AMY RANSACKED MY DESK. THEN THERE BECAUSE EVEN THE SHIT OF TELEPATHY WHAT IS THIS?
EITHER EVERYONE HAS THIS CAPABILITY OR NO, EVERYTHING ELSE IS UNFAIR, SINCE THOUGHTS ARE SUBORDINATED

TO THAT WERE NOT INTENDED. Confidence in the man himself has to build as a person who always understands human behavior without anger only at my husband. But with any uncertainty on my part, a contradictory, it comes to the Push the botton reflex: He would like to go beyond the planet in the air. But I love you all. Then I see the Carefree Cuties. The laugh, happy to have fun. All this, I will. Bother me the not nice Teeth, training tones the body, but the breast is not yet in form. Then I see the horny big boobs teens who have nothing to do with BMW, or that would not be nearly died three months, they laugh, and then more than 14 hours of the best reflection calls. It's all about the feeling.

I WANT AND WHITE: DIRK AND I DO RESEARCH ON, AND BIT BY BIT CLEARS EVERYTHING UP.

THESE LINES ARE CREATED IN A PERIOD IN WHICH NO NEW APARTMENT IS HERE. WHEN WE REFER TO A NEW APARTMENT, SET THEM UP, THEN THE REST COMES BY ITSELF. TEETH AND CHEST.

WHEN I CRY, I FEAR THAT I WILL LOSE DIRK, HE SEES IT SO MUCH THAT I WANT HIM TO GO. HE HAS SO OFTEN GET FROM PEOPLE COMMENTS THAT TO ANNOY BOTH, AS WERE ALSO HELPFUL. ALWAYS MINDFUL ALL POSSIBILITIES WHY MAN NOW SAYS SO HOW HE SAYS IT. DIRK: IF I TELL YOU WHAT, I'LL TELL WHAT. EVERYTHING IS TRUE WHAT I SAY AND WRITE.

I AM BOTH REASON WHY WE WOULD FINANCIAL MUCH FURTHER, IF I DID NOT MAKE MISTAKES CONSTANTLY, BUT ON THE OTHER HAND, I AM REPRESENTATIVE OF ALL PEOPLE THE ONE THAT SOUNDS THE RAGE. I QUESTION, IN ORDER TO CONTRIBUTE TO AN UNDERSTANDING. DIRK TOLD ME SOMETIMES FROM THE PAST, WHAT HE DOES NOT UNDERSTAND TO THIS DAY. SO I LOOK WITH EXPLANATIONS. BUT THAT EXCITES HIM. OR SNEAK THE WORDS: AND YOU OF ALL PEOPLE WANT TO TELL ME THAT? HIS LOVER, ACCURATE, HARMONY CAN ONLY HAPPEN IF THE HUSBAND, (THE COMMON THING WITH GOD MAKES) FINALLY REALIZES THAT 2014 ACTION YEAR HAS STARTED - IE THE SUFFERING IS OVER, IT DOES NO GOOD TO TALK ABOUT THE WICKEDNESS OF MEN, ETC.

BECAUSE I KNOW THAT I EVERYTHING TO ME IS POSSIBLE (FROM PSYCH. VIEW HUMAN AND STAY PLUS) COULD PLAUSIBLY EXPLAINED DIRK. SO I COULD PUT MYSELF IN HIS FATHER'S LIFE MENTALLY, WITH 12 SIBLINGS, PULL NO POSSIBILITY OF DEVELOPMENT, ETC. AND CONCLUSIONS, WHY, WHY HE HAS SO ACTED. THE AIM IS: UNDERSTAND AND THAT PAIN GO AWAY. SO I DO NOT KNOW WHAT ELSE I COULD EXPLAIN WHAT THE PEOPLE HAVE A SET LEFT STANDING THAN SOMEONE IN YOUR OFFICE. THIS DOES NOT MEAN FORGETTING THE CONTRARY. THIS MEANS KNOWLEDGE WITHOUT PAIN. WHY DIRK GETS A HEADACHE WHEN I EXPLAIN? BECAUSE HE IN THIS RESPECT YET A MAN IN THE HEAD NODE HAS DOUBTS - I BLOCK FROM, FOR EXAMPLE, IF I AM TO BE RESPONSIBLE FOR ENSURING

THAT ANY PERSON HAS ACTED OR SO. FIRSTLY: AS LONG AS I DO NOT CONSCIOUSLY OR CHECK THAT NONE OF THE BOOKS, PUBLISHED FROM AN ORDINARY CITIZEN MAKES A SERIAL KILLER SOMETHING AGAINST A MAN, I DINE GOODIES INTO THE COLLECTIVE. EVEN IF THROUGH ME PAMELA ANDERSON NOW WEIGHS ONLY 40 KG, WHICH GIVES ME THE KNOWLEDGE? SHOULD I WRITE TO HER? ENLIGHTEN OR SHOULD I BE BOLD AGAIN, "THICK" AS DIRK HAS THEN SAID TO ME ONCE. CRUEL. WHEN TWO PEOPLE ARE AWARE TO CONTRIBUTE WITH THEIR ACTIONS TO ELIMINATE MISERY IN THE WORLD (DIRKS DAYCARE) IN FUTURE OUR. GODCHILD, THEN THERE ARE ONLY POS. THINGS THAT ARE MOVED BY US AS APPLAUDING THE ROSE. BUT THE SPECIAL EFFECTS RANGE WHICH BRINGS NOTHING. I WANT

TO LAUGH, WITHOUT A HALF-HOUR LATER, THE PAST IS THE SUBJECT LAST. I HAVE PUBLISHED MY SINS ROUGHLY. EVERYONE CAN READ IT. WHAT USE TO ME THAT MY SINS ARE FORGIVEN, IF I'M SO REMINDED WHEN I WAS AT THE LEVEL OF A FEW YEARS AGO? MAN, REJOICE BUT HOW MANY HUSBANDS WOULD BE HAPPY IF YOUR WIFE WITH RESPECT. SEXUALITY WOULD SAY SUCH A THING. YOU'RE A GOOD F.

SO STATEMENTS LIKE STAR..ARE INCOMPREHENSIBLE TO ME, IT SOUNDS TO ME AS IF YOU HOLD A KERSTIN PORN ACTOR. A STAR HALT. DIRK, YOU CAN UNDERSTAND CHARLES MANSON, WHO WAS BY LSD AND ITS SURROUNDINGS INTO A MONSTER, BUT YOU THINK ONLY OF YOUR TRUTH FIRMLY (WITH RESPECT. DIAMETER) BECAUSE YOU THINK YOU WOULD NOT DO THAT, YOU HAD BELIEVE YOU

AND THAT IS SICK? EVERYTHING I WRITE HERE, I'VE ALREADY TOLD ORALLY, BUT IT LEADS TO STRESS. TELL ME UNTIL WE ARE SAFE NO MORE OF OTHERS - OR IF THEN IN REPORT FORM. AT NOON TODAY YOU SAID, WHEN YOU REALIZE THAT MY BEHAVIOR IS LEO BEHAVES DIFFERENTLY ... THE EXAMPLE OF MS. HEINL SITTING SUPPOSEDLY IN JAIL, I CAN UNDERSTAND RELATIONSHIPS, BUT IT DOES NOT HAVE TO SIT THERE BECAUSE OF ME.

A WOMAN WHO IS DEAR, WHAT CAN THAT TELL YOU? PROMPT DOES NOT IN ANY CASE BECAUSE OF PROMPT'S FIRST TAKE A HUGE ANGRY SPEECH. OR WHEN YOU WANTED TO WRITE FOR THE FIRST TIME OBAMA, AND I SAID: YOU DO NOT WRITE, I'M "FLYING" THROUGH THE APARTMENT, THIS WAS ALL RIGHT AFTERWARDS. A WOMAN

WHO IS FOND OF SAYING, YES, OF COURSE, ONLY TIMES THANK, GET THE CHANCE TO DO..ETC. WHAT USE IS LEO, IF HE IS ADORED BY HIS FANS, AND STILL WONDERS IN 500 YEARS AND EVEN ASHS: WHERE IS THE OSCAR, THE WIFE AND THE HAPPINESS. THE OSKAR COMES BY ITSELF, MARRIAGE, THE GERMAN AND HAPPY YOU ARE, IF YOU LISTEN TO DIRK. AND ESPECIALLY IF HE GETS HONEST POST WHERE A MAN TELLS SINCERELY WHAT HE FELT. NO OVER OR UNDERSTATEMENT, ETC. TO EAT DEAD ANIMALS, PERHAPS THE REASON NOT TO REACH THE LEVEL OF HAPPINESS, BECAUSE I WOULD NOT KILL THE ANIMAL TO EAT IT, BUT BUY IT CAPTURES ALL READY, AS YET THE LIE ALREADY ON. OR? AGGRESSIVE IS TRANSMITTED THROUGH THE ANIMAL KINGDOM, SO WHY NOT VEGETARIAN LIFE?

WITH MILK AND EGG PRODUCTS, AND FISH, THAT'S ABSOLUTELY FINE. THE BODY DETOXIFY WELL. GUDD NOW, BREAK.

PART 2

- NOTHING HAPPENED, I SLEPT
WITH REGARD A..
- WITH ANYBODY SEX WITH T
AND 2 PEOPLE - YOU KNOW
- NO PLANNED ASSASSINATION
ATTEMPTS OR UNDERSTANDINGS
OR THOUGHT

PART 3

- GUILTY BECAUSE OF VERBAL STATEMENTS: YOU CAN NOT .. THE
- GIVE ME ONLY THE NUMBER FROM THE VAULT.
- NEGLECT OF ALL THINGS THAT ARE IMPORTANT IN EVERYDAY LIFE
- FAULT IN THE HOUSING CHAOS
- SEX WITH T AND TWO MEN DURING MARRIAGE

PART 4: IT HURTS SO MUCH, DIRK WHERE ARE YOU?

WHERE ARE YOU? I CAN NOT REACH YOU, CELL PHONE MAILBOX. PLEASE GOD, HELP. I HAVE PAIN, PLEASE COME HOME, THE FOOD IS READY, GOD MAKES NO MISTAKES. DIRK PLEASE I'm AFRAID. MY SOUL HURTS SO MUCH. PLEASE COME HOME. I CAN NOT LIVE WITHOUT YOU. LEIDEN, PLEASE COME. I COOKED, CLEANED - SHOWERED - CHATUBATE AND LINDSAY ONGOING AND THE AGONY RIPS ME. I LOVE YOU - NUCLEUS GLOW - NOW I FEEL MY EGOISM, IT HURTS SO MUCH, PLEASE FORGIVE ME. NO HASSLE ANGER MORE TALK, I YEARN TO TALK OH GOD, I AM ASHAMED THE NEW HOME IS BEAUTIFUL, AND WE READ THEIR BOOKS TOGETHER - WHERE ARE YOU? WHY IS OFF THE PHONE? ONLY WITH YOU I CAN REALLY TALK, I

DEEPLY REGRET INSENSITIVITY AND THAT I'M STILL NOT BREAST, BEAUTIFUL TEETH AND TAUT. LOVE FLOWS FROM ME, HOPEFULLY YOU WILL RECEIVE IT. YOU MIGHT BE MORE SHOPPING - WHY IS THIS PHONE? AS IN NIGHTMARES. NO MATTER WHERE WE LIVE, I JUST WANT TO YOU - GO GOD AND GODDESS BY KAISERSLAUTERN - GO SHOPPING. MY THOUGHTS ARE ALWAYS FULL OF LOVE, BUT THE WRATH OF GOD - MAN, WE HAVE FOR ETERNITY MARRIED, IMMORTALITY WITHOUT SUFFERING, ANGER AND GRIEF - THE BLACK RED BOOK, BECAUSE WE PLAN TO WRITE ON, WHICH IS NICE. PLEASE COME HOME. I WILL NO LONGER BE SO INSENSITIVE, PLEASE LET US OPEN OUR SOUL AND HEART. GOD PLEASE GIVE ME A CHANCE, I NEED DIRK - JUST WHERE YOU ARE IS MY HOME. CRUEL, AT EVERY SOUND I

THINK YOU'RE AT THE DOOR. And I HAVE YOU THEN DAYS LEFT ALONE, THAT'S SO BRUTAL, OH GOD, PLEASE COME HOME, WE FALL INTO HIS ARMS AND FEEL OUR LOVE - I'M LOST IN THE MOMENT, DO NOT KNOW ANYTHING MORE. NOW I HAVE TO THINK OF THE EVIL VOICES THAT SAY THAT NO LONGER COMES, WHO HAS TAKEN THE MONEY AND GONE -

THIS IS NOT POSSIBLE. AND AGAIN THE FEAR IS WHAT HAPPENS THAT HURTS SO MUCH. AGAIN WENT PEOPLE AT STOREFRONT, I HEARD A BUNCH OF KEYS, I THOUGHT YOU WERE THERE, BUT THEY WERE NEIGHBORS. OH GOD, I NEVER WANT TO DO AGAIN WHAT THAT DIRK UPSET IF HE WERE ONLY HERE. I MISS YOU - THERE ARE NOW MORE THAN THREE HOURS, YOU WANTED ..DU'RE DAA I AM THE HAPPIEST HUMAN +

ESPECIALLY I THANK MY
HUSBAND

www.ingramcontent.com/pod-product-compliance
Lightning Source LLC
Chambersburg PA
CBHW072252310526
45795CB00011B/1083